Gorgeous
Cakes

Gorgeous
Cakes

for the ultimate sweet sensation

First published in 2010
LOVE FOOD is an imprint of Parragon Books Ltd

Parragon
Queen Street House
4 Queen Street
Bath BA1 1HE, UK

ISBN: 978-1-4454-0438-7

Printed in China

Notes for the Reader
This book uses imperial, metric, and US cup measurements. Follow the same units of measurement throughout; do not mix imperial and metric. All spoon measurements are level: teaspoons are assumed to be 5 ml, and tablespoons are assumed to be 15 ml. Unless otherwise stated, milk is assumed to be whole and eggs are medium.

The times given are an approximate guide only. Preparation times differ according to the techniques used by different people and the cooking times may also vary from those given as a result of the type of oven used. Optional ingredients, variations, or serving suggestions have not been included in the calculations.

Recipes using raw or very lightly cooked eggs should be avoided by infants, the elderly, pregnant women, convalescents, and anyone with a chronic condition. Pregnant and breast-feeding women are advised to avoid eating peanuts and peanut products. People with nut allergies should be aware that some of the prepared ingredients used in the recipes in this book may contain nuts. Always check the packaging before use.

PICTURE ACKNOWLEDGMENTS
The publisher would like to thank the following for permission to reproduce copyright material. Front cover image: Victoria Sponge © Steve Baxter/Getty Images

For front cover recipe, please see page 10.

Contents

Introduction

Nothing can beat the sight and taste of a freshly baked cake. Even if you're not a domestic god or goddess, the good news is that homemade cakes don't have to be difficult or time-consuming. This book is packed with delicious cakes for all occasions, so you'll never be short of ideas for easy, irresistible home-baked treats.

Few types of cooking offer more rewards than home baking. Not only can you make superb cakes for your family and friends, but the actual hands-on process of baking is immensely satisfying and you'll be surprised by how much fun it can be.

The basic skills of cake making are really easy to learn and you need very little in the way of special equipment to make some impressive cakes. The equipment needed for baking cakes can be found in most kitchens: mixing bowl, flour sifter, measuring cups and spoons, wire rack, and cake pans. Good-quality cake pans conduct heat evenly and efficiently for perfect results and will last for years. Because cake pan sizes vary between manufacturers, some of the recipes in this book provide the pan's capacity. To find a pan's capacity, simply use a measuring cup to pour water into the pan and note how much liquid it takes to fill the pan.

Follow the top tips on the opposite page to ensure perfect results and you'll soon realize there is no time like the present to dig out your apron, get baking, and rediscover the joy of an afternoon's cake making!

•Turn on the oven before you start in order to preheat it to the correct temperature while you're mixing.

•Brush cake pans with melted butter or oil and line with nonstick parchment paper to prevent sticking.

•Always use eggs at room temperature. If you store eggs in the refrigerator, remove them about 30 minutes before use to let them reach room temperature.

•Avoid overmixing because this can cause a heavy texture—beat the batter until just smooth.

•Bake the cake immediately once mixed because the baking powder begins to act as soon as it's combined with liquid.

•Avoid opening the oven during cooking—this reduces the oven temperature and can cause cakes to sink.

•Test cakes carefully for doneness—they should be well risen, golden brown, and starting to shrink from the sides of the pan. Sponge cakes should feel springy to the touch.

Everyday Cakes

Vanilla Sponge Layer Cake

serves 6–8

oil or melted butter,
for greasing

1½ cups all-purpose flour

1 tbsp baking powder

¾ cup unsalted butter,
softened

generous ¾ cup superfine
sugar

3 eggs, beaten

1 tsp vanilla extract

2 tbsp milk

filling

¼ cup unsalted butter,
softened

1 cup confectioners' sugar,
plus extra for dusting

½ tsp vanilla extract

3 tbsp strawberry jelly

Preheat the oven to 350°F/180°C. Grease two 8-inch/20-cm layer cake pans and line the bottoms with parchment paper.

Sift the flour and baking powder into a large bowl and add the butter, superfine sugar, eggs, and vanilla extract. Beat well until the batter is smooth, then stir in the milk.

Divide the batter between the prepared pans and smooth level. Bake in the preheated oven for 25–30 minutes, or until risen, firm, and golden brown. Let cool in the pans for 2–3 minutes, then turn out onto a wire rack to finish cooling.

For the filling, beat together the butter, confectioners' sugar, and vanilla extract until smooth. Spread this mixture on top of one of the cakes. Spread the bottom of the other cake with the jelly and then sandwich the two cakes together to enclose the filling, pressing down lightly. Dust the cake with confectioners' sugar before serving.

Angel Food Cake

serves 10

oil or melted butter,
for greasing
1 cup all-purpose flour, plus
extra for dusting
8 extra-large egg whites
1 tsp cream of tartar
1 tsp almond extract
1¼ cups superfine sugar

topping
2¼ cups berries, such as
strawberries and raspberries
1 tbsp lemon juice
2 tbsp confectioners' sugar

Preheat the oven to 325°F/160°C. Brush the inside of a 7½-cup angel cake pan with oil and dust lightly with flour.

In a large grease-free bowl, whisk the egg whites until they hold soft peaks. Add the cream of tartar and whisk again until the whites are stiff but not dry.

Whisk in the almond extract, then add the sugar a tablespoon at a time, whisking hard between each addition. Sift in the flour and fold in lightly and evenly using a large metal spoon.

Spoon the batter into the prepared cake pan and tap on the counter to remove any large air bubbles. Bake in the preheated oven for 40–45 minutes, or until golden brown and firm to the touch.

Run the tip of a small knife around the edge of the cake to loosen from the pan. Let cool in the pan for 10 minutes, then turn out onto a wire rack to finish cooling.

For the topping, place the berries, lemon juice, and confectioners' sugar in a saucepan and heat gently until the sugar has dissolved. Place on top of the cake.

Frosted Carrot Cake

serves 16

oil or melted butter,
for greasing
¾ cup sunflower oil
¾ cup light brown sugar
3 eggs, beaten
1¼ cups grated carrots
⅔ cup golden raisins
½ cup walnut pieces
grated rind of 1 orange
1½ cups self-rising flour
1 tsp baking soda
1 tsp ground cinnamon
½ tsp grated nutmeg
strips of orange zest,
to decorate

frosting

scant 1 cup cream cheese
scant 1 cup confectioners'
sugar
2 tsp orange juice

Preheat the oven to 350°F/180°C. Grease a 9-inch/23-cm square cake pan and line the bottom with parchment paper.

In a large bowl, beat the oil, brown sugar, and eggs together. Stir in the carrots, golden raisins, walnuts, and orange rind.

Sift together the flour, baking soda, cinnamon, and nutmeg, then stir evenly into the carrot mixture.

Spoon the batter into the prepared cake pan and bake in the preheated oven for 40–45 minutes, until well risen and firm to the touch. Let cool in the pan for 5 minutes, then turn out onto a wire rack to finish cooling.

For the frosting, combine the cream cheese, confectioners' sugar, and orange juice in a bowl and beat until smooth. Spread over the cake and swirl with a spatula. Decorate with strips of orange zest, cut into squares, and serve.

Lemon Drizzle Cake

serves 8

oil or melted butter,
for greasing
1¾ cups all-purpose flour
2 tsp baking powder
1 cup superfine sugar
4 eggs
⅔ cup sour cream
grated rind of 1 large lemon
4 tbsp lemon juice
⅔ cup sunflower oil

syrup
¼ cup confectioners' sugar
3 tbsp lemon juice

Preheat the oven to 350°F/180°C. Grease an 8-inch/20-cm loose-bottom round cake pan and line the bottom with parchment paper.

Sift the flour and baking powder into a mixing bowl and stir in the superfine sugar. In a separate bowl, whisk the eggs, sour cream, lemon rind, lemon juice, and oil together. Pour the egg mixture into the dry ingredients and mix well until evenly combined.

Pour the batter into the prepared pan and bake in the preheated oven for 45–60 minutes, or until risen and golden brown.

For the syrup, mix together the confectioners' sugar and lemon juice in a small pan. Stir over low heat until just beginning to bubble and turn syrupy.

As soon as the cake comes out of the oven, prick the surface with a fine skewer, then brush the syrup over the top. Let the cake cool completely in the pan before turning out and serving.

Hummingbird Cake

serves 10

oil or melted butter,
for greasing
2¼ cups all-purpose flour
1¼ cups superfine sugar
1 tsp ground cinnamon
1 tsp baking soda
3 eggs, beaten
scant 1 cup sunflower oil
scant 1 cup pecans, coarsely
chopped, plus extra
to decorate
1 cup mashed ripe bananas
(about 3 bananas)
3 oz/85 g canned crushed
pineapple (drained weight),
plus 4 tbsp juice from
the can

filling and frosting
¾ cup cream cheese
4 tbsp unsalted butter
1 tsp vanilla extract
3½ cups confectioners' sugar

Preheat the oven to 350°F/180°C. Grease three 9-inch/23-cm layer cake pans and line the bottoms with parchment paper.

Sift together the flour, superfine sugar, cinnamon, and baking soda into a large bowl. Add the eggs, oil, pecans, bananas, pineapple, and pineapple juice and stir with a wooden spoon until evenly mixed.

Divide the batter among the prepared pans and smooth level. Bake in the preheated oven for 25–30 minutes, or until golden brown and firm to the touch.

Remove the cakes from the oven and let cool in the pans for 10 minutes, then turn out onto wire racks to finish cooling.

For the filling and frosting, beat together the cream cheese, butter, and vanilla extract in a bowl until smooth. Sift in the confectioners' sugar and mix until smooth.

Sandwich the cakes together with half of the mixture, spread the remaining frosting over the top, then sprinkle with pecans to decorate.

Classic Cherry Cake

serves 8

oil or melted butter,
for greasing
generous 1 cup candied
cherries, quartered
¾ cup ground almonds
1¾ cups all-purpose flour
1 tsp baking powder
scant 1 cup butter
1 cup superfine sugar
3 extra-large eggs
finely grated rind and juice
of 1 lemon
6 sugar cubes, crushed

Preheat the oven to 350°F/180°C. Grease an 8-inch/20-cm round cake pan and line with parchment paper.

Stir together the candied cherries, ground almonds, and 1 tablespoon of the flour. Sift the remaining flour into a separate bowl with the baking powder.

Cream together the butter and superfine sugar until light in color and fluffy in texture. Gradually add the eggs, beating hard with each addition, until evenly mixed.

Add the flour mixture and fold lightly and evenly into the creamed mixture with a metal spoon. Add the cherry mixture and fold in evenly. Finally, fold in the lemon rind and juice.

Spoon the batter into the prepared cake pan and sprinkle with the crushed sugar cubes. Bake in the preheated oven for 1–1¼ hours, or until risen, golden brown, and the cake is just beginning to shrink away from the sides of the pan.

Let cool in the pan for 15 minutes, then turn out onto a wire rack to finish cooling.

Rich Fruitcake

serves 16

scant 2½ cups golden raisins

1⅔ cups raisins

½ cup chopped plumped
dried apricots

½ cup chopped pitted dates

4 tbsp dark rum or brandy,
plus extra for flavoring
(optional)

finely grated rind and juice of
1 orange

1 cup butter, plus extra
for greasing

1 cup light brown sugar

4 eggs

generous ⅓ cup chopped
candied peel

⅓ cup candied cherries,
quartered

2 tbsp chopped candied
ginger or preserved ginger

⅓ cup chopped blanched
almonds

1¾ cups all-purpose flour

1 tsp apple pie spice

Place the golden raisins, raisins, apricots, and dates in a large bowl and stir in the rum, orange rind, and orange juice. Cover and let soak for several hours or overnight.

Preheat the oven to 300°F/180°C. Grease a deep 8-inch/20-cm round cake pan and line the bottom with parchment paper.

Cream together the butter and sugar until light and fluffy. Gradually beat in the eggs, beating hard after each addition. Stir in the soaked fruits, candied peel, candied cherries, candied ginger, and blanched almonds.

Sift together the flour and apple pie spice, then fold lightly and evenly into the batter. Spoon into the prepared cake pan and level the surface, making a slight depression in the center with the back of the spoon.

Bake in the preheated oven for 2¼–2¾ hours, or until the cake is beginning to shrink away from the sides of the pan and a toothpick inserted into the center comes out clean. Cool completely in the pan.

Turn out the cake and remove the lining paper. Wrap with wax paper and foil, and store for at least 2 months before use. To add a richer flavor, prick the cake with a toothpick and spoon over a couple of tablespoons of rum or brandy, if using, before storing.

Coffee & Walnut Cake

serves 8

oil or melted butter,
for greasing
¾ cup butter
¾ cup light brown sugar
3 extra-large eggs, beaten
3 tbsp strong black coffee
1½ cups self-rising flour
1½ tsp baking powder
1 cup walnut pieces
walnut halves,
to decorate

filling and frosting
½ cup butter
1¾ cups confectioners' sugar
1 tbsp strong black coffee
½ tsp vanilla extract

Preheat the oven to 350°F/180°C. Grease two 8-inch/20-cm layer cake pans and line the bottoms with parchment paper.

Cream together the butter and brown sugar until pale and fluffy. Gradually add the eggs, beating well after each addition. Beat in the coffee.

Sift the flour and baking powder into the batter, then fold in lightly and evenly with a metal spoon. Fold in the walnut pieces.

Divide the batter between the prepared cake pans and smooth level. Bake in the preheated oven for 20–25 minutes, or until golden brown and springy to the touch. Let cool in the pans for 5 minutes, then turn out onto wire racks to finish cooling.

For the filling and frosting, beat together the butter, confectioners' sugar, coffee, and vanilla extract, mixing until smooth and creamy.

Use about half the mixture to sandwich the cakes together, then spread the remaining buttercream on top and swirl with a metal spatula. Decorate with walnut halves.

Chocolate Fudge Cake

serves 8

oil or melted butter,
for greasing

2 oz/55 g semisweet
chocolate

2 tbsp milk

1½ cups all-purpose flour

1 tbsp baking powder

¾ cup unsalted butter,
softened

generous ¾ cup dark brown
sugar

3 eggs, beaten

1 tsp vanilla extract

grated chocolate, to decorate

filling and frosting

3½ oz/100 g semisweet
chocolate

4 tbsp unsalted butter,
softened

1½ cups confectioners' sugar

1 tsp vanilla extract

1 tbsp milk

Preheat the oven to 350°F/180°C. Grease a 9-inch/23-cm round cake pan and line with parchment paper.

Put the chocolate and milk into a small saucepan and heat gently until melted, without boiling. Remove from the heat.

Sift the flour and baking powder into a large bowl and add the butter, brown sugar, eggs, and vanilla extract. Beat well until smooth, then stir in the melted chocolate mixture, mixing evenly.

Spoon the batter into the prepared pan and smooth level. Bake in the preheated oven for 50–60 minutes, or until firm to the touch and just beginning to shrink away from the sides of the pan.

Let cool in the pan for 10 minutes, then turn out onto wire racks to finish cooling. When cold, carefully slice the cake horizontally into 2 layers.

For the filling and frosting, melt the chocolate with the butter in a small pan over low heat. Remove from the heat and stir in the confectioners' sugar, vanilla extract, and milk, then beat well until smooth.

Sandwich the cake layers together with half the chocolate mixture, then spread the remainder on top of the cake, swirling with a spatula. Sprinkle with the grated chocolate before serving.

Chocolate Sandwich Cake

serves 8

oil or melted butter,
for greasing

1⅓ cups all-purpose flour

2 tbsp unsweetened cocoa

1 tbsp baking powder

¾ cup unsalted butter,
softened

generous ¾ cup superfine
sugar

3 eggs, beaten

1 tsp vanilla extract

2 tbsp milk

⅔ cup chocolate spread

confectioners' sugar,
for dusting

Preheat the oven to 350°F/180°C. Grease two 8-inch/20-cm layer cake pans and line the bottoms with parchment paper.

Sift the flour, cocoa, and baking powder into a large bowl and add the butter, superfine sugar, eggs, and vanilla extract. Beat well until the mixture is smooth, then stir in the milk.

Divide the batter between the prepared pans and smooth level. Bake in the preheated oven for 25–30 minutes, or until golden brown and firm to the touch. Let cool in the pans for 2–3 minutes, then turn out onto a wire rack to finish cooling.

When the cakes have cooled completely, sandwich them together with the chocolate spread, then dust with confectioners' sugar and serve.

Celebration Cakes

Dotty Chocolate Chip Cake

serves 10

oil or melted butter,
for greasing

¾ cup soft margarine
or softened butter

scant 1 cup superfine sugar

3 eggs, beaten

1½ cups all-purpose flour

1½ tsp baking powder

2 tbsp unsweetened cocoa

⅓ cup white chocolate chips

1½ oz/40 g small colored
candies, to decorate

frosting

6 oz/175 g milk chocolate or
semisweet chocolate

7 tbsp unsalted butter
or margarine

1 tbsp dark corn syrup

Preheat the oven to 325°F/170°C. Grease an 8-inch/20-cm round cake pan and line the bottom with parchment paper.

Place the margarine, sugar, eggs, flour, baking powder, and cocoa in a bowl and beat until just smooth. Stir in the chocolate chips, mixing evenly.

Spoon the batter into the prepared pan and smooth level. Bake in the preheated oven for 40–45 minutes, until risen and firm to the touch. Let cool in the pan for 5 minutes, then turn out onto a wire rack to finish cooling.

For the frosting, place the chocolate, butter, and corn syrup in a saucepan over low heat and stir until just melted and smooth.

Remove from the heat and let cool until it begins to thicken enough to leave a trail when the spoon is lifted. Pour the frosting over the top of the cake, letting it drizzle down the sides. Arrange the candies over the top of the cake.

Birthday Lemon Sponge Cake

serves 8–10

oil or melted butter,
for greasing

generous 1 cup unsalted
butter

1¼ cups superfine sugar

4 eggs, beaten

2¼ cups self-rising flour

finely grated rind of 1 lemon

3 tbsp milk

filling and frosting

10 tbsp unsalted butter

1¾ cups confectioners'
sugar

2 tbsp lemon juice or lemon
liqueur (Limoncello)

3 tbsp lemon curd

Preheat the oven to 350°F/180°C. Grease two 8-inch/20-cm layer cake pans and line the bottoms with parchment paper.

Cream together the butter and superfine sugar until pale and fluffy. Gradually add the eggs, beating well after each addition. Sift in the flour and fold in evenly with a metal spoon. Fold in the lemon rind and milk lightly and evenly.

Spoon the batter into the prepared pans and bake in the preheated oven for 25–30 minutes, or until golden brown and springy to the touch. Let the cakes cool in the pans for 2–3 minutes, then turn out onto a wire rack to finish cooling.

For the frosting, beat together the butter, confectioners' sugar, and lemon juice until smooth. For the filling, mix about 3 tablespoons of the frosting with the lemon curd. Use the lemon curd mixture to sandwich the two cakes together.

Spread about two-thirds of the remaining buttercream over the top of the cake, swirling with a spatula. Spoon the remainder into a pastry bag and pipe swirls around the edge of the cake. Add candleholders and birthday candles to finish.

Rose Gâteau

serves 8–10

oil or melted butter, for greasing

1½ cups all-purpose flour

1 tbsp baking powder

¾ cup unsalted butter, softened

generous ¾ cup superfine sugar

3 eggs, beaten

1 tsp rose water

2 tbsp milk

filling and icing

⅔ cup heavy cream

1 tsp rose water

1¾ cups confectioners' sugar, sifted

to decorate

fresh rose petals, washed and patted dry

½ egg white

superfine sugar, for sprinkling

Preheat the oven to 350°F/180°C. Grease two 9-inch/23-cm layer cake pans and line the bottoms with parchment paper.

Sift the flour and baking powder into a large bowl and add the butter, superfine sugar, eggs, and rose water. Beat well until the mixture is smooth, then stir in the milk.

Divide the mixture between the prepared pans and smooth level. Bake in the preheated oven for 25–30 minutes, or until risen, firm, and golden brown. Let cool in the pans for 2–3 minutes, then turn out and onto a wire rack to finish cooling.

For the filling, whip the cream with ½ teaspoon of the rose water until just thick enough to hold its shape. Use to sandwich the cakes together.

For the icing, combine the confectioners' sugar with the remaining rose water and just enough water to mix to a thick pouring consistency. Spoon it over the cake, letting it drizzle down the sides. Let set.

Brush the rose petals with the egg white, sprinkle with superfine sugar, and arrange on top of the cake to decorate.

Marbled Pastel Cake

serves 12

oil or melted butter,
for greasing

1½ cups all-purpose flour

1 tbsp baking powder

¾ cup unsalted butter,
softened

generous ¾ cup superfine
sugar

3 eggs, beaten

1 tsp vanilla extract

2 tbsp milk

pink edible food coloring

1 lb 9 oz/700 g ready-to-use
rolled fondant

3 tbsp apricot jelly, warmed

sugar flowers, to decorate

Preheat the oven to 325°F/160°C. Grease a deep 9-inch/23-cm round cake pan and line with parchment paper.

Sift the flour and baking powder into a large bowl and add the butter, sugar, eggs, and vanilla extract. Beat well until the mixture is smooth, then stir in the milk. Spoon half the mixture into a separate bowl and stir in a few drops of food coloring.

Spoon alternate tablespoonfuls of the two mixtures into the prepared pan and swirl lightly with a spatula for a marbled effect.

Bake in the preheated oven for 40–50 minutes, or until risen, firm, and golden brown. Let cool in the pan for 10 minutes, then turn out onto a wire rack to finish cooling.

Divide the fondant in half and knead a few drops of food coloring into one half. Place the white and pink mixtures together and knead together for a marbled effect.

Place the cake on a board, brush with apricot jelly, and roll out the fondant to cover the cake. Trim the edges, then roll the trimmings into 2 long ropes, twist together, and place around the bottom of the cake. Decorate with sugar flowers.

Bumblebee Cake

serves 8–10

oil or melted butter,
for greasing

generous 2 cups all-purpose
flour

1 tbsp baking powder

¾ cup unsalted butter,
softened

generous ¾ cup superfine
sugar

3 eggs, beaten

1 tsp vanilla extract

2 tbsp lemon juice

finely grated rind of 1 lemon

filling and frosting

¾ cup unsalted butter

2¼ cups confectioners' sugar,
sifted

3 tbsp honey

2 tbsp lemon juice

to decorate

9 oz/250 g white ready-to-
use rolled fondant

a few drops of yellow and
black edible food colorings

Preheat the oven to 325°F/160°C. Grease a 6¾-cup heatproof bowl.

Sift the flour and baking powder into a bowl and add the butter, superfine sugar, eggs, and vanilla extract. Beat well until smooth, then stir in the lemon juice and rind.

Spoon the mixture into the prepared bowl and smooth level. Bake in the preheated oven for 1¼–1½ hours, or until risen, firm, and golden brown. Let cool for 5 minutes in the bowl, then turn out onto a wire rack to finish cooling.

For the filling and frosting, beat together the butter, confectioners' sugar, honey, and lemon juice until smooth. Slice the cake horizontally into 3 layers. Use about a quarter of the buttercream to sandwich the layers together.

Using a pastry bag fitted with a large plain tip, pipe the remaining frosting in lines around the cake to resemble a beehive.

Reserve a quarter of the white fondant, then color half the remainder yellow and half black. Shape to make small bees, making the wings from the white fondant and attaching with a dab of water. Press the bees into the frosting.

Valentine Chocolate Heart Cake

serves 12

oil or melted butter,
for greasing

1½ cups self-rising flour

2 tsp baking powder

½ cup unsweetened cocoa

3 eggs

scant ¾ cup light brown sugar

⅔ cup sunflower oil

⅔ cup light cream

fresh mint sprigs, to decorate

filling and topping

8 oz/225 g semisweet
chocolate

generous 1 cup heavy cream

3 tbsp seedless raspberry jelly

generous 1 cup fresh or frozen
raspberries

Preheat the oven to 350°F/180°C. Grease an 8-inch/20-cm wide heart-shape cake pan and line the bottom with parchment paper.

Sift the flour, baking powder, and cocoa into a large bowl. Beat the eggs with the sugar, oil, and light cream. Make a well in the dry ingredients and add the egg mixture, then stir to mix thoroughly, beating to a smooth batter.

Pour the batter into the prepared pan and bake in the preheated oven for 25–30 minutes, or until risen and firm to the touch. Cool in the pan for 10 minutes, then turn out onto a wire rack to finish cooling.

For the filling and topping, place the chocolate and heavy cream in a saucepan over low heat and stir until melted. Remove from the heat and stir until the mixture cools slightly and begins to thicken.

Use a sharp knife to cut the cake in half horizontally. Spread the cut surface of each half with the raspberry jelly, then top with about 3 tablespoons of the chocolate mixture. Sprinkle on half the raspberries and replace the top, pressing down lightly.

Spread the remaining chocolate mixture over the top and sides of the cake, swirling with a spatula. Top with the remaining raspberries and decorate with mint sprigs.

Easter Marzipan Fruitcake

serves 16

oil or melted butter,
for greasing

¾ cup unsalted butter

scant 1 cup light brown sugar

3 eggs, beaten

2 cups all-purpose flour

½ tsp baking powder

2 tsp apple pie spice

finely grated rind of 1 small
lemon

scant ½ cup currants

scant ¾ cup golden raisins

⅓ cup chopped candied peel

1 lb 9 oz/700 g marzipan

3 tbsp apricot jelly

Preheat the oven to 300°F/150°C. Grease a deep 8-inch/20-cm round cake pan and line with parchment paper.

Place the butter and sugar in a bowl and cream together until pale, light, and fluffy. Gradually beat in the eggs, beating hard after each addition. Sift together the flour, baking powder, and apple pie spice. Use a large metal spoon to fold into the creamed mixture. Stir in the lemon rind, currants, golden raisins, and candied peel, mixing evenly. Spoon half the batter into the prepared pan and smooth level.

Roll out about one-third of the marzipan to an 8-inch/20-cm round and place over the batter in the pan. Add the remaining cake batter and smooth level. Bake the cake in the preheated oven for 2¼–2¾ hours, or until firm and golden and the sides are beginning to shrink away from the pan. Let cool in the pan for 30 minutes, then turn out onto a wire rack to finish cooling.

Brush the top of the cake with apricot jelly. Roll out two-thirds of the remaining marzipan to a round to cover the top of the cake. Use a knife to mark a lattice design in the surface and pinch the edges to decorate.

Roll the remaining marzipan into eleven small balls and arrange around the edge of the cake. Place under a hot broiler for 30–40 seconds to brown lightly. Cool before storing.

Halloween Pumpkin Cake

serves 10

oil or melted butter,
for greasing

1½ cups all-purpose flour

1 tbsp baking powder

1 tsp pumpkin pie spice

¾ cup unsalted butter,
softened

generous ¾ cup light brown
sugar

3 eggs, beaten

1 tsp vanilla extract

1½ cups coarsely grated
pumpkin flesh

to decorate

3 tbsp apricot jelly, warmed

a few drops of orange and
black edible food colorings

1 lb 12 oz/800 g ready-to-use
rolled fondant

black, green, and yellow
writing icing

Preheat the oven to 325°F/160°C. Grease a deep 9-inch/23-cm round cake pan and line with parchment paper.

Sift the flour, baking powder, and pumpkin pie spice into a bowl and add the butter, sugar, eggs, and vanilla extract. Beat well until smooth, then stir in the pumpkin.

Spoon the batter into the prepared cake pan and smooth level. Bake in the preheated oven for 40–50 minutes, or until well risen, firm, and golden brown. Let cool in the pan for 10 minutes, then turn out onto a wire rack to finish cooling.

Brush the cake with the warmed apricot jelly. Knead orange food coloring into about three-quarters of the fondant and roll out to cover the top and sides of the cake. Trim the edges neatly, reserving the trimmings.

Form the trimmings into small pumpkin shapes, then use the black writing icing to pipe faces and the green writing icing to pipe stalks onto them. Knead black food coloring into the remaining fondant, then roll it out and cut into bat shapes. Pipe eyes onto the bats using yellow writing icing, then place the pumpkins and bats onto the cake to decorate.

Golden Christmas Cake

serves 16–18

¾ cup chopped dried apricots

⅓ cup chopped dried mango

⅓ cup chopped
dried pineapple

generous 1 cup golden raisins

¼ cup chopped
preserved ginger

⅓ cup chopped candied peel

finely grated rind and juice of
1 orange

4 tbsp brandy

¾ cup unsalted butter, plus
extra for greasing

½ cup light brown sugar

4 eggs, beaten

2 tbsp honey

1½ cups self-rising flour

2 tsp ground allspice

¾ cup pecans

to decorate, (optional)

1 lb 12 oz/800 g marzipan

2 lb/900 g ready-to-use rolled
fondant

silver dragées

Place the chopped apricots, mango, and pineapple in a bowl with the golden raisins, preserved ginger, and candied peel. Stir in the orange rind, orange juice, and brandy. Cover the bowl and let soak overnight.

Preheat the oven to 325°F/170°C. Grease a 9-inch/23-cm round springform cake pan and line with parchment paper.

Cream together the butter and brown sugar until the mixture is pale and fluffy. Add the eggs, beating well between each addition. Stir in the honey.

Sift the flour with the allspice and fold into the mixture using a metal spoon. Add the soaked fruit and pecans, stirring thoroughly to mix. Spoon the batter into the prepared pan, spreading it evenly, then make a slight dip in the center.

Place the pan in the center of the preheated oven and bake for 1½–2 hours, or until golden brown and firm to the touch and a toothpick inserted into the center comes out clean. Let cool in the pan.

Turn the cake out, remove the lining paper, and rewrap in clean parchment paper and foil. Store in a cool place for at least 1 month before use. If you want, cover the cake with marzipan and fondant, following the package instructions, and decorate with silver dragées.

Christmas Mulled Sponge Loaf

serves 8

oil or melted butter,
for greasing

1½ cups all-purpose flour

1 tbsp baking powder

1 tsp apple pie spice

¾ cup unsalted butter,
softened

generous ¾ cup light brown
sugar

3 eggs, beaten

1 tsp vanilla extract

finely grated rind of 1 orange

2 tbsp orange juice

syrup

⅔ cup confectioners' sugar

scant ½ cup port or red wine

1 piece of star anise

to decorate

10 fresh cranberries

10 fresh bay leaves

1 egg white

3 tbsp superfine sugar

Preheat the oven to 350°F/180°C. Grease a 5-cup loaf pan and line with parchment paper.

Sift the flour, baking powder, and apple pie spice into a large bowl and add the butter, brown sugar, eggs, and vanilla extract. Beat well until the mixture is smooth, then stir in the orange rind and juice.

Spoon the batter into the prepared pan and smooth level. Bake in the preheated oven for 40–50 minutes, or until risen, firm, and golden brown. (Don't worry if the cake dips slightly in the center.)

Remove the pan from the oven and stand it on a wire rack. For the syrup, put the confectioners' sugar, port, and star anise into a pan and heat gently until boiling. Boil rapidly for 2–3 minutes to reduce slightly. Remove the star anise.

·Spoon the syrup over the cake and let soak for 30 minutes. Turn out the cake from the pan, upside down.

Brush the cranberries and bay leaves with the egg white and sprinkle with the superfine sugar, then arrange on top of the cake.

Something Different

Caribbean Coconut Cake

serves 10

oil or melted butter,
for greasing

¾ cup butter, softened

scant 1 cup superfine sugar

3 eggs

1¼ cups self-rising flour

1½ tsp baking powder

½ tsp freshly grated nutmeg

⅔ cup dry unsweetened
coconut

2 tbsp coconut cream

toasted dry unsweetened
coconut, to decorate

filling and frosting

2¾ cups confectioners' sugar

½ cup butter

3 tbsp coconut cream

5 tbsp pineapple jelly

Preheat the oven to 350°F/180°C. Grease two 8-inch/20-cm round layer cake pans and line the bottoms with parchment paper.

Place the butter in a bowl with the superfine sugar and eggs and sift in the flour, baking powder, and nutmeg. Beat together until smooth, then stir in the coconut and the coconut cream.

Divide the batter between the prepared pans and smooth level. Bake in the preheated oven for 25 minutes, or until golden and firm to the touch. Let cool in the pans for 5 minutes, then turn out onto a wire rack to finish cooling.

For the filling and frosting, sift the confectioners' sugar into a bowl and add the butter and coconut cream. Beat together until smooth. Spread the pineapple jelly on one of the cakes and top with just under half of the buttercream. Place the other cake on top. Spread the remaining buttercream on top of the cake and scatter with the toasted coconut.

Pineapple Upside-Down Cake

serves 10

oil or melted butter
for greasing
4 eggs, beaten
1 cup superfine sugar
1 tsp vanilla extract
1¾ cups all-purpose flour
2 tsp baking powder
generous ½ cup unsalted
butter, melted

topping
3 tbsp unsalted butter
4 tbsp dark corn syrup
15 oz/425 g canned pineapple
rings, drained
4–6 candied cherries, halved

Preheat the oven to 325°F/160°C. Grease a deep 9-inch/23-cm round cake pan with a solid bottom and line the bottom with parchment paper.

For the topping, place the butter and corn syrup in a heavy-bottom pan and heat gently until melted. Bring to a boil and boil for 2–3 minutes, stirring, until slightly thickened and taffylike.

Pour the syrup into the bottom of the prepared pan. Arrange the pineapple rings and candied cherries in a single layer over the syrup.

Place the eggs, sugar, and vanilla extract in a large heatproof bowl set over a saucepan of gently simmering water and beat with an electric mixer for 10–15 minutes, until thick enough to leave a trail when the beater is lifted. Sift in the flour and baking powder and fold in lightly and evenly with a metal spoon.

Fold the melted butter into the batter with a metal spoon until evenly mixed. Spoon into the prepared pan and bake in the preheated oven for 1–1¼ hours, or until well risen, firm, and golden brown.

Let cool in the pan for 10 minutes, then carefully turn out onto a serving plate. Serve warm or cold.

Orange & Poppy Seed Bundt Cake

serves 10

oil or melted butter,
for greasing

2¼ cups all-purpose flour,
plus extra for dusting

scant 1 cup unsalted butter

1 cup superfine sugar

3 extra-large eggs, beaten

finely grated rind of 1 orange

¼ cup poppy seeds

2 tsp baking powder

⅔ cup milk

½ cup orange juice

strips of orange zest, to
decorate

syrup

scant ¾ cup superfine sugar

⅔ cup orange juice

Preheat the oven to 325°F/160°C. Grease and lightly flour an 8¾-cup tube pan.

Cream together the butter and sugar until pale and fluffy, then add the eggs gradually, beating thoroughly after each addition. Stir in the orange rind and poppy seeds. Sift in the flour and baking powder, then fold in evenly. Add the milk and orange juice, stirring evenly to mix.

Spoon the batter into the prepared pan and bake in the preheated oven for 45–50 minutes, or until firm and golden brown. Cool in the pan for 10 minutes, then turn out onto a wire rack to finish cooling.

For the syrup, place the sugar and orange juice in a saucepan and heat gently until the sugar melts. Bring to a boil and simmer for about 5 minutes, until reduced and syrupy.

Spoon the syrup over the cake while it is still warm. Top with the strips of orange zest and serve warm or cold.

Applesauce Cake

serves 6

oil or melted butter,
for greasing
1½ cups all-purpose flour
1 tbsp cornstarch
1 tbsp baking powder
¾ cup unsalted butter,
softened
generous ¾ cup superfine
sugar, plus extra for sprinkling
3 eggs, beaten
1 tsp vanilla extract
scant 1 cup applesauce or
thick apple puree
1 apple
lemon juice, for brushing

Preheat the oven to 350°F/180°C. Grease two 8-inch/20-cm layer cake pans and line the bottoms with parchment paper.

Sift the flour, cornstarch, and baking powder into a large bowl and add the butter, sugar, eggs, and vanilla extract. Beat well until the mixture is smooth. Stir in ⅓ cup of the applesauce.

Divide the batter between the prepared pans and smooth level. Bake in the preheated oven for 25–30 minutes, or until risen, firm, and golden brown.

Let cool in the pans for 5 minutes, then turn out onto a wire rack to finish cooling. Use the remaining applesauce to sandwich the cakes together.

Core and thinly slice the apple and brush with lemon juice. Arrange the slices on top of the cake to decorate, then sprinkle with a little superfine sugar.

Glazed Fruit & Nut Cake

serves 16–18

oil or melted butter,
for greasing

2¼ cups all-purpose flour,
plus extra for dusting

1 tbsp baking powder

1 tsp apple pie spice

¾ cup unsalted butter,
softened

generous ¾ cup dark brown
sugar

3 eggs, beaten

1 tsp vanilla extract

2 tbsp milk

2 cups mixed dried fruit

¾ cup chopped mixed nuts

to decorate

3 tbsp honey, warmed

1½ cups mixed candied fruits,
such as pineapple,
cherries, and orange

½ cup whole shelled nuts,
such as Brazil nuts,
almonds, and walnuts

Preheat the oven to 325°F/160°C. Grease a 9-inch/23-cm round springform cake pan and dust lightly with flour.

Sift the flour, baking powder, and apple pie spice into a large bowl and add the butter, sugar, eggs, and vanilla extract. Beat well until the mixture is smooth, then stir in the milk, mixed dried fruit, and chopped nuts.

Spoon the batter into the prepared pan and smooth level. Bake in the preheated oven for about 1 hour, or until risen, firm, and golden brown.

Let cool in the pan for 30 minutes, then remove the sides and place on a wire rack to finish cooling.

Brush the top of the cake with a little of the warmed honey, then arrange the candied fruits and whole nuts on top. Brush with the remaining honey and let set.

Mocha Layer Cake

serves 8

oil or melted butter,
for greasing
1¾ cups self-rising flour
¼ tsp baking powder
4 tbsp unsweetened cocoa
½ cup superfine sugar
2 eggs
2 tbsp corn syrup
⅔ cup sunflower oil
⅔ cup milk

filling and topping
1 tsp instant coffee powder
1 tbsp boiling water
1¼ cups heavy cream
2 tbsp confectioners' sugar

to decorate
1¾ oz/50 g chocolate, grated
marbled chocolate caraque
confectioners' sugar,
for dusting

Preheat the oven to 350°F/180°C. Grease three 7-inch/18-cm layer cake pans and line with parchment paper.

Sift the flour, baking powder, and unsweetened cocoa into a large mixing bowl. Stir in the superfine sugar. Make a well in the center and stir in the eggs, corn syrup, oil, and milk. Beat with a wooden spoon, gradually mixing in the dry ingredients to make a smooth batter.

Divide the cake batter among the prepared pans. Bake in the preheated oven for 35–45 minutes, or until springy to the touch. Let cool in the pans for 5 minutes, then turn out onto a wire rack to finish cooling.

For the filling and topping, dissolve the instant coffee in the boiling water and place in a bowl with the cream and confectioners' sugar. Whip until the cream is just holding its shape. Use half of the cream to sandwich the 3 cakes together. Spread the remaining cream over the top and sides of the cake.

To decorate, lightly press the grated chocolate into the cream around the edge of the cake. Transfer to a serving plate. Lay the caraque over the top of the cake. Cut a few thin strips of parchment paper and place on top of the caraque. Dust lightly with confectioners' sugar, then carefully remove the paper.

Rich Chocolate Rum Torte

serves 8

oil or melted butter,
for greasing

2½ oz/70 g semisweet
chocolate

2 tbsp milk

1½ cups all-purpose flour

1 tbsp baking powder

¾ cup unsalted butter,
softened

generous ¾ cup dark brown
sugar

3 eggs, beaten

1 tsp vanilla extract

chocolate curls or grated
chocolate, to decorate

filling and frosting

8 oz/225 g semisweet
chocolate

1 cup heavy cream

2 tbsp dark rum

Preheat the oven to 350°F/180°C. Grease three 7-inch/18-cm layer cake pans and line the bottoms with parchment paper.

Put the chocolate and milk into a small pan and heat gently, without boiling, until melted. Stir and remove from the heat.

Sift the flour and baking powder into a large bowl and add the butter, sugar, eggs, and vanilla extract. Beat well until smooth, then stir in the chocolate mixture.

Divide the cake batter among the prepared pans and smooth level. Bake in the preheated oven for 20–25 minutes, or until risen and firm to the touch.

Let cool in the pans for 5 minutes, then turn out onto wire racks to finish cooling.

For the filling and frosting, melt the chocolate with the cream and rum in a small pan over low heat. Remove from the heat and let cool, stirring occasionally, until it reaches a spreadable consistency.

Sandwich the cakes together with about a third of the chocolate mixture, then spread the remainder over the top and sides of the cake, swirling with a spatula. Sprinkle with chocolate curls and let set.

Chocolate Ganache Cake

serves 10

oil or melted butter,
for greasing

¾ cup unsalted butter

¾ cup superfine sugar

4 eggs, lightly beaten

1¾ cups self-rising flour

1 tbsp unsweetened cocoa

1¾ oz/50 g semisweet
chocolate, melted

7 oz/200 g chocolate-flavored
confectionery coating,
to decorate

ganache

2 cups heavy cream

13 oz/375 g semisweet
chocolate, broken into pieces

Preheat the oven to 350°F/180°C. Grease an 8-inch/20-cm springform cake pan and line with parchment paper.

Beat the butter and sugar together in a bowl until light and fluffy. Gradually add the eggs, beating well after each addition. Sift the flour and unsweetened cocoa together, then fold into the cake batter. Fold in the melted chocolate.

Pour into the prepared pan and smooth level. Bake in the preheated oven for 40 minutes, or until springy to the touch. Let the cake cool for 5 minutes in the pan, then turn out onto a wire rack to finish cooling. Cut the cake into 2 layers.

For the ganache, place the cream in a saucepan and bring to a boil, stirring. Add the chocolate and stir until melted. Pour into a bowl, cool, then chill for 2 hours, or until set and firm. Whisk the mixture until light and fluffy and set aside. Reserve one-third of the ganache. Use the rest to sandwich the cake together and spread over the cake.

Melt the confectionery coating and spread it over a large sheet of parchment paper. Let cool until just set. Cut into strips a little wider than the height of the cake. Place the strips around the edge of the cake, overlapping them slightly.

Pipe the reserved ganache in teardrops or shells to cover the top of the cake. Let chill for 1 hour.

Chocolate & Almond Layer Cake

serves 10–12

oil or melted butter,
for greasing
7 eggs
1¾ cups superfine sugar
1¼ cups all-purpose flour
½ cup unsweetened cocoa
4 tbsp butter, melted

filling and topping
7 oz/200 g semisweet dark
chocolate
½ cup butter
4 tbsp confectioners' sugar

to decorate
10 tbsp toasted slivered
almonds, crushed lightly
grated chocolate

Preheat the oven to 350°F/180°C. Grease a deep 9-inch/23-cm square cake pan and line the bottom with parchment paper.

Beat the eggs and superfine sugar in a mixing bowl with an electric mixer for about 10 minutes, or until the batter is very light and foamy and the beaters leave a trail that lasts a few seconds when lifted.

Sift the flour and cocoa together and fold half into the batter. Drizzle over the melted butter and fold in the rest of the flour and cocoa. Pour into the prepared pan and bake in a preheated oven for 30–35 minutes, or until springy to the touch. Let cool in the pan for 5 minutes, then turn out onto a wire rack to finish cooling.

For the filling and topping, melt the chocolate and butter together, then remove from the heat. Stir in the confectioners' sugar and let cool, then beat until thick enough to spread.

Halve the cake lengthwise and cut each half into 3 layers. Sandwich the layers together with three-quarters of the chocolate mixture. Spread the remainder over the cake and mark a wavy pattern on the top. Press the almonds onto the sides. Decorate with grated chocolate.

Stollen

⅔ cup lukewarm milk

¼ cup superfine sugar

2 tsp active dry yeast

2½ cups white bread flour

½ tsp salt

½ cup butter, softened, plus extra for greasing

1 medium egg, beaten

¼ cup currants

⅓ cup golden raisins

⅓ cup finely diced candied peel

¼ cup candied cherries

3 tbsp chopped, blanched almonds

grated rind of ½ lemon

6 oz/175 g marzipan, formed into a 9-inch/23-cm sausage

icing

1 cup confectioners' sugar, sifted

1 tbsp water

Pour the warm milk into a small bowl, add 1 teaspoon of the sugar, sprinkle in the yeast, and whisk thoroughly. Set aside for 10 minutes, until a frothy head has formed.

Set aside 2 tablespoons of flour and sift the rest into a large mixing bowl with the salt and remaining sugar. Make a well in the center, pour in the yeast mixture, then add the butter and beaten egg. Mix well to form a soft dough.

Work in the currants, raisins, peel, cherries, almonds, and lemon rind, then transfer the dough to a counter and knead for 5 minutes, until smooth and elastic. Place in a clean bowl, cover with plastic wrap, and let stand in a warm place for 1½–2 hours, until doubled in size.

Sprinkle the reserved flour onto a counter and turn out the dough onto it. Punch out the air, then knead again until smooth and elastic. Roll out to a 10 x 8-inch/25 x 20-cm rectangle and place the marzipan in the center. Grease a baking sheet. Fold the remaining dough over the marzipan and place, seam-side down, on the prepared baking sheet. Cover and set aside until doubled in size. Meanwhile, preheat the oven to 375°F/190°C.

Bake in the preheated oven for 35–40 minutes, until risen and golden. Transfer to a wire rack to cool slightly. Mix the confectioners' sugar with the warm water and spread it thinly over the stollen while it is still warm. Cut into slices and serve.

Dessert Cakes

New York Cheesecake

serves 10

generous ½ cup butter, plus
extra for greasing

1¾ cups finely crushed
graham crackers

1 tbsp granulated sugar

4 cups cream cheese

1¼ cups superfine sugar

2 tbsp all-purpose flour

1 tsp vanilla extract

finely grated zest of 1 orange

finely grated zest of 1 lemon

3 eggs

2 egg yolks

1¼ cups heavy cream

Preheat the oven to 350°F/180°C. Place a small saucepan over low heat, add the butter, and heat until it melts, then remove from the heat, stir in the crushed graham crackers and sugar, and mix thoroughly. Press the crumb mixture tightly into the bottom of a 9-inch/23-cm springform cake pan. Place in the oven and bake for 10 minutes. Remove from the oven and let cool on a wire rack.

Increase the oven temperature to 400°F/200°C. With an electric mixer, beat the cream cheese until creamy, then gradually add the sugar and flour and beat until smooth. Increase the speed and beat in the vanilla extract, orange zest, and lemon zest, then beat in the eggs and egg yolks one at a time. Finally, beat in the cream. Scrape any excess from the sides and beaters of the mixer into the mixture. It should be light and whippy—beat on a faster setting if you need to.

Grease the sides of the cake pan and pour in the filling. Smooth the top, transfer to the preheated oven, and bake for 15 minutes, then reduce the temperature to 200°F/100°C and bake for an additional 30 minutes. Turn off the oven and let the cheesecake stand in it for 2 hours to cool and set. Cover and refrigerate overnight.

Orange Cheesecake Gâteau

serves 8–10

oil or melted butter,
for greasing

1½ cups all-purpose flour

1 tbsp baking powder

¾ cup unsalted butter,
softened

generous ¾ cup superfine
sugar

3 eggs, beaten

1 tsp orange flower water

2 tbsp orange juice

filling and topping

1 lb 5 oz/600 g mascarpone
cheese

finely grated rind of 1 orange

4 tbsp orange juice

½ cup confectioners' sugar

1 tsp orange flower water

decorate

1 orange, peeled and sliced

maple syrup, for brushing

Preheat the oven to 350°F/180°C. Grease two 9-inch/23-cm layer cake pans and line with parchment paper.

Sift the flour and baking powder into a large bowl and add the butter, superfine sugar, eggs, and orange flower water. Beat well until the mixture is smooth, then stir in the orange juice.

Divide the mixture between the prepared pans and smooth level. Bake in the preheated oven for 25–30 minutes, or until risen and golden brown. Let cool in the pans for 5 minutes, then turn out onto a wire rack to finish cooling.

For the filling and topping, beat together all the ingredients until smooth and spread about a third over one cake. Spoon the remainder into a pastry bag fitted with a large star tip and pipe swirls around the edge.

Place the second cake on top. Pipe the remaining frosting around the top edge. Fill the center with orange slices and brush with maple syrup.

Citrus Mousse Cake

serves 12

oil or melted butter,
for greasing
¾ cup butter
¾ cup superfine sugar
4 eggs, lightly beaten
1¾ cups self-rising flour
1 tbsp unsweetened cocoa
1¾ oz/50 g orange-flavored
semisweet chocolate, melted
peeled orange segments,
to decorate

filling and topping
2 eggs, separated
4 tbsp superfine sugar
¾ cup freshly squeezed
orange juice
2 tsp gelatin
3 tbsp water
1¼ cups heavy cream

Preheat the oven to 350°F/180°C. Grease an 8-inch/20-cm round springform cake pan and line the bottom with parchment paper.

Beat the butter and sugar in a bowl until light and fluffy. Gradually add the eggs, beating well after each addition. Sift together the flour and cocoa and then fold into the creamed mixture. Fold in the melted chocolate. Pour into the prepared pan and smooth level. Bake in the preheated oven for 40 minutes, or until springy to the touch. Let cool for 5 minutes in the pan, then turn out onto a wire rack and let cool completely. Cut the cold cake into two layers.

For the filling, beat the egg yolks and sugar until pale, then beat in the orange juice. Sprinkle the gelatin over the water in a small heatproof bowl and let it go spongy, then place over a saucepan of hot water and stir until dissolved. Stir into the egg yolk mixture.

Whip the cream until holding its shape. Reserve a little for decoration and fold the remainder into the mousse. Beat the egg whites until standing in soft peaks, then fold in. Let stand in a cool place until starting to set, stirring occasionally.

Place one half of the cake in the pan. Pour in the mousse and press the second half of the cake on top. Chill until set. Transfer to a plate, then spoon teaspoonfuls of cream around the top and arrange orange segments in the center.

Strawberry Mousse Cake

serves 8–10

oil or melted butter,
for greasing

1½ cups all-purpose flour

1 tbsp baking powder

¾ cup unsalted butter,
softened

generous ¾ cup superfine
sugar

3 eggs, beaten

1 tsp vanilla extract

2 tbsp milk

filling and topping

4 tsp powdered gelatin

3 tbsp orange juice

5 cups fresh strawberries

3 tbsp superfine sugar

1½ cups heavy cream

scant ½ cup grape jelly,
warmed

Preheat the oven to 325°F/160°C. Grease a 9-inch/23-cm round springform cake pan and line with parchment paper.

Sift the flour and baking powder into a large bowl and add the butter, sugar, eggs, and vanilla extract. Beat well until the batter is smooth, then stir in the milk.

Spoon the batter into the prepared pan and smooth level. Bake in the preheated oven for 45–55 minutes, or until risen and golden brown.

Let cool in the pan for 5 minutes, then turn out onto a wire rack to finish cooling. Cut the cake in half horizontally and place half back in the cake pan.

For the filling, dissolve the gelatin in the orange juice in a small bowl placed in a pan of hot water. In a blender or processor, puree 3½ cups of the strawberries with the sugar. Whip the cream until thick enough to hold its shape. Quickly stir the gelatin into the strawberry mixture, then fold in the cream.

Pour the mixture into the pan and place the second half of the cake on top. Chill in the refrigerator until set. Turn out the cake and spread the top with warmed grape jelly. Decorate with the remaining strawberries.

Meringue-Topped Coffee Liqueur Cake

serves 6–8

oil or melted butter, for greasing

1½ cups all-purpose flour

1 tbsp baking powder

¾ cup unsalted butter, softened

generous ¾ cup light brown sugar

3 eggs, beaten

1 tsp coffee extract

2 tbsp milk

3 tbsp coffee liqueur

meringue topping

3 egg whites

¾ cup superfine sugar

1½ tsp coffee extract

Preheat the oven to 325°F/160°C. Grease a 10-inch/25-cm round cake pan and line with parchment paper.

Sift the flour and baking powder into a large bowl and add the butter, brown sugar, eggs, and coffee extract. Beat well until the batter is smooth, then stir in the milk.

Spoon the batter into the prepared pan and smooth level. Bake in the preheated oven for 40–50 minutes, or until risen, firm, and golden brown.

Let cool in the pan for 2–3 minutes, then turn out onto a flameproof serving plate. Prick the cake all over with a skewer, then sprinkle with the liqueur.

For the meringue topping, put the egg whites into a clean bowl and beat with an electric handheld mixer until thick enough to hold soft peaks. Gradually add the superfine sugar, beating vigorously after each addition, then beat in the coffee extract.

Spoon the meringue on top of the cake and spread into peaks and swirls with a spatula. Use a chef's blowtorch to brown the meringue, or place the cake under a hot broiler for 2–3 minutes, or until just browned but still soft inside. Cut into slices and serve.

Chocolate & Cherry Gâteau

serves 8

oil or melted butter,
for greasing

1⅓ cups all-purpose flour

2 tbsp unsweetened cocoa

1 tbsp baking powder

¾ cup unsalted butter,
softened

generous ¾ cup superfine
sugar

3 eggs, beaten

1 tsp vanilla extract

2 tbsp milk

3 tbsp Kirsch or brandy
(optional)

grated chocolate and fresh
whole cherries, to decorate

filling and topping

2 cups heavy cream

2 tbsp confectioners' sugar

1⅓ cups fresh or frozen pitted
black cherries

Preheat the oven to 350°F/180°C. Grease two 8-inch/20-cm layer cake pans and line the bottoms with parchment paper.

Sift the flour, cocoa, and baking powder into a large bowl and add the butter, superfine sugar, eggs, and vanilla extract. Beat well until the mixture is smooth and stir in the milk.

Divide the mixture between the prepared pans and smooth level. Bake in the preheated oven for 25–30 minutes, or until risen and firm to the touch. Let cool in the pans for 2–3 minutes, then turn out onto wire racks to finish cooling.

When the cakes are cold, sprinkle with the Kirsch, if using. Whip the cream with the confectioners' sugar until thick, then spread about a third over the top of one of the cakes. Spread the cherries over the cream mixture and place the second cake on top.

Spread the remaining cream mixture over the top and sides of the cake and decorate with grated chocolate and fresh whole cherries.

Double Chocolate Mint Sponge

serves 8

oil or melted butter,
for greasing

generous 1¼ cups
all-purpose flour

2 tbsp unsweetened cocoa

1 tbsp baking powder

¾ cup unsalted butter,
softened

scant 1 cup superfine sugar

3 eggs, beaten

1 tbsp milk

12 chocolate mint sticks,
chopped

⅔ cup chocolate spread,
plus extra to drizzle

chocolate mint sticks
to decorate

Preheat the oven to 350°F/180°C. Grease two 8-inch/20-cm layer cake pans and line the bottoms with parchment paper.

Sift the flour, unsweetened cocoa, and baking powder into a bowl and beat in the butter, sugar, and eggs, mixing until smooth. Stir in the milk and chocolate mint pieces.

Spread the batter into the pans. Bake for 25–30 minutes, until risen and firm. Cool in the pan for 2 minutes, then turn out onto a wire rack to finish cooling.

Sandwich the cakes together with the chocolate spread, then drizzle more chocolate spread over the top. Decorate the cake with chocolate mint sticks.

Deep Chocolate Cheesecake

serves 6–8

oil or melted butter,
for greasing

1⅓ cups finely crushed
graham crackers

2 tsp unsweetened cocoa

4 tbsp butter, melted

chocolate leaves,
to decorate

filling

1 lb 12 oz/800 g mascarpone
cheese

scant 2 cups confectioners'
sugar, sifted

juice of ½ orange

finely grated rind of
1 orange

6 oz/175 g semisweet
chocolate, melted

2 tbsp cognac

Grease an 8-inch/20-cm loose-bottom round cake pan.

Put the crushed graham crackers, cocoa, and melted butter into a large bowl and mix well. Press the crumb mixture evenly over the bottom of the prepared pan.

For the filling, put the mascarpone cheese and confectioners' sugar into a bowl and stir in the orange juice and rind. Add the melted chocolate and cognac and mix together until thoroughly combined. Spread the chocolate mixture evenly over the crumb layer. Cover with plastic wrap and let chill for at least 4 hours.

Remove the cheesecake from the refrigerator, turn out onto a serving plate, and decorate with chocolate leaves before serving.

Hot Chocolate Cheesecake

oil or melted butter,
for greasing

scant 1½ cups all-purpose
flour

2 tbsp unsweetened cocoa

4 tbsp butter, plus extra
for greasing

2 tbsp superfine sugar

¼ cup ground almonds

1 egg yolk

confectioners' sugar and
grated chocolate, to decorate

filling

2 eggs, separated

scant ½ cup superfine sugar

1½ cups cream cheese

4 tbsp ground almonds

⅔ cup heavy cream

¼ cup unsweetened cocoa,
sifted

1 tsp vanilla extract

Grease an 8-inch/20-cm loose-bottom round cake pan.

Sift the flour and cocoa into a bowl and rub in the butter until the mixture resembles fine breadcrumbs. Stir in the sugar and ground almonds. Add the egg yolk and enough water to make a soft dough.

Roll the pastry out on a lightly floured work surface and use to line the prepared pan. Let chill for 30 minutes. Preheat the oven to 325°F/160°C.

For the filling, put the egg yolks and sugar in a large bowl and beat until thick and pale. Beat in the cream cheese, ground almonds, cream, cocoa, and vanilla extract until well combined.

Put the egg whites in a large bowl and beat until stiff but not dry. Stir a little of the egg white into the cream cheese mixture, then fold in the remainder. Pour into the pastry shell.

Bake in the preheated oven for 1½ hours, until well risen and just firm to the touch. Carefully remove from the pan, dust with confectioners' sugar, and sprinkle with grated chocolate. Serve warm.

Chocolate Cake with Syrup

serves 12

oil or melted butter,
for greasing

8 oz/225 g semisweet
chocolate, broken
into pieces

½ cup butter

1 tbsp strong black coffee

4 large eggs

2 egg yolks

⅔ cup superfine sugar

½ cup all-purpose flour

2 tsp ground cinnamon

1 cup ground almonds

chocolate-covered coffee
beans, to decorate

syrup

1¼ cups strong black coffee

⅔ cup superfine sugar

1 cinnamon stick

Preheat the oven to 375°F/190°C. Grease an 8-inch/20-cm round cake pan and line with parchment paper.

Place the chocolate, butter, and coffee in a heatproof bowl and set over a saucepan of gently simmering water until melted. Stir to blend, then remove from the heat and let cool slightly.

Place the whole eggs, egg yolks, and sugar in a separate bowl and beat together until thick and pale. Sift the flour and cinnamon over the egg mixture. Add the almonds and the chocolate mixture and fold in carefully. Spoon the cake batter into the prepared pan. Bake in the preheated oven for 35 minutes, or until the tip of a knife inserted into the center comes out clean. Let cool slightly before turning out onto a serving plate.

For the syrup, place the coffee, sugar, and cinnamon stick in a heavy-bottom pan and heat gently, stirring, until the sugar has dissolved. Increase the heat and boil for 5 minutes, or until reduced and thickened slightly. Keep warm. Pierce the surface of the cake with a skewer, then drizzle half the coffee syrup over the top. Decorate with chocolate-covered coffee beans. Cut into wedges, drizzle with remaining coffee syrup, and serve.